HOW TO
MAKE
YOUR LIFE
COUNT

*Life is not measured by the number of
breaths we take but by the number of
moments that take our breath away.*

-Unknown

HERITAGE PRESS

P.O. Box HCU, Florence, AL 35630

HOW TO MAKE YOUR LIFE COUNT

ISBN 978-0-9772414-0-8, Printed in the U.S.A.

For more information, visit www.hcu.edu.

HOW TO MAKE YOUR LIFE COUNT

DENNIS JONES

HERITAGE PRESS

P.O. Box HCU, Florence, AL 35630

&~ ~ *Dedication* ~ &

To my family, my coworkers, and the many audiences who patiently have listened to me over the years...

and

To those of you who want to leave the world in better shape than you found it.

❧ Acknowledgements ❧

A special thanks to the faculty, staff, and students at Heritage Christian University for their constant inspiration and encouragement.

Thanks to my assistant, Alana Marks, for her unselfish efforts to help make me an author.

Thank you to Cory Collins, Sara Goldman, and Lori Eastep for their proofreading suggestions on the numerous drafts of the manuscript.

And an extra special thanks to Dr. Betty Hamblen for the countless hours spent patiently correcting, editing, and rewriting this manuscript.

Table of Contents

Introduction

❧❧You Can Spend It Only Once❧❧

> *Many people's tombstones should read*
> *"Died at 30, buried at 80"*
> --Nicholas Murray Butler

In his book *Walden* Henry David Thoreau makes the following statement: "The mass of men lead lives of quiet desperation." When I first read that statement as a young man, I did not believe it. Surely, the people that I saw around me everyday were not desperate. Certainly, the great number of people in my state, in my country, and in the world could not be leading lives of desperation.

But the years have taught me a lot, and I think now I know what he meant. I think he meant that most people don't know what their lives are about. They quietly go about working, playing, eating, and existing from day to day. In actuality, however, their work and relationships don't give them a sense of fulfillment. They don't display joy in what they do. In fact, they really don't know what they are supposed to be doing. They can't say, "I fit exactly where I am now. This is the place, the work, the arena that I need to be in. I can see my purpose here."

I believe that the majority of people have the *Paper Cup in the Parking Lot* syndrome. Someone throws a paper cup out the window of the car. It rolls around the parking lot as the wind blows it first one way and then the other. The

1

wind changes direction and the paper cup tumbles the other way. Then a gust of wind picks it up and deposits it on the other side of the parking lot. A car comes by and blows the cup near the curb. Another car pushes it back into the lot. Finally a big truck roars close and "squash" goes the paper cup.

Many people live their lives that way. Whatever happens to them happens to them. *"Que Sera, Sera"* the old song says... whatever will be, will be. Those people don't have a direction. They don't have a feeling of purpose. And they certainly don't have an understanding of the meaning of their lives. They drift from one job to another and from one relationship to another. They have no sense of intentional living. They use up time, space, and energy as they "blow" from here to there. Eventually, they drift to old age and then "squash", it is over. Theirs are lives of quiet desperation.

THE REST OF YOUR LIFE

If you are reading this book, then you have already determined that you do not want to live your life that way. Some of you are at the starting gate of adulthood. Life still looks new and exciting. You are beginning to build families and jumpstart your careers. It's hard for you even to see down the path of time to the end of your years.

Others of you are in the middle years with responsibilities crowding from every direction. You have children in a whirlwind of activities. You have aging parents with needs and demands. Your careers are in full swing, and churches and communities desperately need your leadership and involvement. You often feel pulled in all directions by the demands of family, work, church, and civic responsibilities. You are probably expecting many more decades of life to come, but already you are beginning to sense that the end will come sooner than you want. You are feeling your mortality.

Some of you may be in the midst of the autumn years. You may even be approaching the heavy winter season of your life. You are beginning to see more years in your past than you can see in your future. Life has slowed down. Careers have halted and children have grown up and left home. Demands from the community and from church have relented, but you are still expecting to live a while longer in activity and service.

Whatever your age is now, whether you are in your teens or in your 80s, you still have the *rest* of your life to live. The important question for all of us at any age, as we consider the life ahead, is, "What will I do with it?"

An old proverb states, "Life is like a coin. You can spend it any way you want, but you can only spend it once." Because we have only one opportunity at life, we need to spend our "coin" on something valuable. We will not get another coin or another chance to re-spend it. Therefore, that life/coin needs to count. It needs to make a difference. The only way a life can make a difference is for it to have purpose and meaning.

MAKING YOUR LIFE COUNT

How do you make your life count?

While I don't claim to be an expert, my role as a university president has put me in a unique position. God, by His grace, has allowed me to be in contact with thousands of people all over the world.

I have met community leaders, church members, and students from every walk of life. They are the exceedingly wealthy as well as the extremely poor. Some hold top leadership positions and others are unemployed. I have conversed with the academically privileged and those who never finished high school. Many are multitalented performers and others are the "Johnny One-Notes".

I have observed something interesting as I have met this cross-section of humanity. I have observed that socioeconomic group, job status, or leadership position has little impact on purpose of life. Some people, regardless of circumstances, status, or material goods, leave a deep impression on life, while others drift through each day like dried leaves in a stream.

The ones in the second group have failed to grasp the reasons for their existence. They seem to think that climbing the corporate ladder, having meaningful relationships, and attaining material possessions are the purposes of their lives. They seem to be the desperate ones that Thoreau mentioned.

On the other hand, those in the first group have made their lives count for something. They have a sense of purpose. Their lives have meaning. Some of them have made their way into this book. They have been my teachers in how to make a difference in life. They have grasped a few basic principles that seem to elude the majority of the population. How did they do it?

Through the years of observation, I have noted that almost anyone with any kind of background can make his life count... *if* that person will adhere to eight principles. The good news is that everybody can learn all eight of them.

No matter who you are, no matter what your economic status is, and no matter whether you are at the

4

bottom or at the top of the totem pole, you do not have to lead a life of quiet desperation. Your life can have meaning and purpose. You can leave an impression on life. The people who will follow in years to come will know that you have been here.

The rest of this book will introduce you to the eight principles that anybody can do to make a difference. Those eight things are not rocket science. In fact, they are not difficult at all. Not one of the eight is beyond anyone's ability to understand and apply.

Fully grasp all of the eight principles and make them your own. As you live them each day, you will notice your life taking on purpose and meaning. Your life will begin to have an impact on other lives it touches. It will begin to make a difference. You *can* make your life count.

John 6:47

Most assuredly, I say to you, he who believes in Me has everlasting life.

In the next few pages you will discover that:

- ❖ The idea of eternal life is essential to your life.
- ❖ God gives eternal life as a gift .
- ❖ Understanding the concept of everlasting life guides your life in the here and now.

Principle One

৯৯Believe You Will Live Forever৯৯

There is a fundamental concept that seems to mark a divide between youth and adulthood. As a young person grows, he thinks that he is invincible. He is going to live forever, and he will be young and strong always.

That same young person steps over into "grown-up" land, however, when he first realizes that his body will grow, age, and eventually die. He is not invincible, and he will not live forever. When he realizes and understands that concept, then he no longer looks at time or life as a child does.

To those of you who want to live a worthwhile and noteworthy life I suggest that you need to believe exactly the opposite! In order to live a life that counts, you must *believe with all your heart that you will live... FOREVER.*

Obviously, I do not want you to believe that your body will live forever. That goes against all human reason and experience. But you must believe that you--the real you-- are eternal. You are not a body with a soul, but you are a spirit temporarily housed in a body.

"God has put eternity in their hearts," said Solomon in Ecclesiastes 3:11. When God created you and me, He programmed eternity into us. That means that we are built to last. We will last, not just for 70 or 80 years, but for eternity.

You must believe that, even though your body will decay with age and cease to exist, death will not be the end for you. The real you, the spirit, will continue after your temporary "house" dies. You will live forever.

7

EVERLASTING LIFE

Most teachers know that repetition is a key to learning. Good teachers make sure their students repeat many times the letters of the alphabet. They ask them numerous times to say by rote the numbers in the multiplication table. Bible class teachers go over and over with their students the names of books of the Bible. Teachers even make up songs or poems to help children learn by repetition. They know that the things they are learning are basic to the study of language, math and the Scriptures. Thus, they have the students master the basics by repetition.

I have noticed that the Master Teacher also used repetition. He often made an important statement and then repeated it several times. That repetition seems to indicate that He wanted us to learn whatever concept He mentioned—that it is a basic concept and important.

With that in mind, notice this statement in John 6:40: "And this is the will of Him who sent Me, that everyone who sees the Son and believes in Him may have *everlasting life*; and I will raise him up at the last day." This same idea is repeated in verse 47. "Most assuredly, I say to you, he who believes in Me has everlasting life," and in verse 51, "I am the living bread which came down from heaven. If anyone eats of this bread, he will *live forever...*" Then He repeats the same words in verses 54 and 58.

Through the repetition of this concept, Jesus indicates that the idea of eternal life and the means of obtaining it are so basic and important that they must be ingrained into our hearts and minds.

YOU HAVE A RESERVATION

Scripture indicates that eternal life is a gift of God in Christ Jesus (Romans 6:23). This means that at the moment of your conception, God created you as an eternal being that will never cease to exist.

Eternal life is a gift given to all mankind, but those who are followers of Christ have a special gift. Not only will they live forever, but they will live forever in a special place. In fact, they already have a reservation there because their names are written in the Book of Life.

I travel often on business for the university. On a few occasions when I have arrived at the hotel much later than my originally scheduled time, I have been severely disappointed. When I tried to check in at the desk, the clerk told me that they did not think I would show up, so THEY SOLD MY ROOM!

On those occasions, I have not been the smiling, friendly person I usually am. I once asked the check-in attendant. "If the President of the United States showed up right now, could you find a room for him?"

She reluctantly admitted, "Well, yeah, I guess."

"Well," I said. "He's not coming. I'll take his room!"

To another clerk who told me she had sold my room, I replied, "All right, but I'm sleeping in the lobby and I want you to know that I sleep in ragged pajamas!" She found me a room.

On a cold and rainy night, when all you want is to reach that cozy, warm room and fall into peaceful sleep, what a disappointment it is when you find that you have no reservation. But, oh, it is sweet comfort to walk into a lobby, give your name to the clerk, and hear him say, "Welcome. We've been expecting you. Your name is right here on our reservation list."

If you are in Christ, which means obedient to Him, you will not be disappointed by not having a room. Your reservation is already made. (Hebrews 12:23) When you get to heaven, you will be welcome because your name is registered there... not just for an overnight, temporary stay, but for eternity.

You are an eternal being. To make your life count, that belief is basic.

HOW THIS CONCEPT MAKES A DIFFERENCE

But what difference does it make if you believe you will live forever?

If you believe with all your heart that you are an eternal being, you will view your earthly life through a long-range viewfinder. You will make decisions and assess your life with the knowledge that you are forever. In fact, you may completely change some decisions you have already made. You will begin to look at people, events, and circumstances through the range of years. You will be concerned with long-term benefits. You will have different goals. Priorities will shift.

Many years ago when I was young and going through a particularly difficult and vulnerable period, I had a friend who repeatedly told me, "Don't do anything that you will regret in 100 years." At the time I did not think that statement was helpful. After all, I was not hurting tomorrow or next week or in 100 years. I was hurting right then! I needed help then, not in some distant future.

10

With the perspective of years, and with more understanding of Christ, I know without a doubt that my friend was absolutely correct. What you do today really *will* matter 100 years from now.

A woman who decides to become involved in encouraging and counseling a needy friend may impact the future of that friend and even succeeding generations. A Bible teacher who decides to take one of his troubled students under his wing can influence for decades the spiritual direction of that student's entire family. A young adult who decides to become a Christian will have influence that reaches beyond her lifetime. Thousands may eventually be in heaven because of her one, timely decision.

Conversely, an angry man who impetuously decides to pick up a gun and take another's life may suffer consequences of his reckless action for scores of years. But his quick decision affects not only his life but the lives of his family members through future generations.

Decisions that you make today may have effects that reach beyond 100 or even 1,000 years. The person who believes that he will live forever understands that and so manages his measured amount of earthly time with that in mind.

Believe that you will live forever and let it change your life.

A Hundred Years from Now

Tell me, friend, what will it matter
A hundred years from now
If you owned ten thousand acres
Or just a broken plow;
If you bought your suits in Paris
And your clothes in Italy
Or your clothes were made in patches
As the bed quilts used to be;
Whether you lived in a mansion
With the finest broadlooms laid,
If you had a private chauffeur,
Butler, cook, and maid?
Or if you lived in a cottage
With your health gone on the skids,
Out of work and with no money,
Just your wife and seven kids?
Yes, there's more to life than living,
More for those who will believe,
More in store laid up in Heaven
If the Savior we receive.
Whether we are lost forever
Or to Jesus here we bow–
This is what will make a difference
A hundred years from now.

-Author Unknown

James 4:14

What is your life? It is even a vapor that appears for a little time and then vanishes away.

In the next few pages you will discover that:

❖ You do not need to fear death.

❖ You will win the battle with death.

❖ You must savor your life as you do the last cookie of the bunch.

Principle Two

ᕱᕲᕲAccept Your Mortality ᕲᕲᕲ

> *Here lies Ezekial Aikle*
> *Age 102*
> *The good die young*
> --Epitaph, East Dolhousie
> Cemetery, Nova Scotia

We chuckle at that epitaph, but the truth is that most of us would like to have a similar statement made about us. Whenever we die, I suspect that most of us will feel that death came much too early.

To many people death is a fearful subject. They don't want to talk about or think about death and certainly do not wish to consider their own death. But those who want to make their lives count must think about the end of life.

About this time, you may be saying, "Now hold on. Didn't you just say in the last chapter that we must believe we will live forever?" Yes, I did.

This second important principle of making life count may seem to contradict everything you just read in the last chapter, but stay with me as I explain. You can only make your life count if you accept and get comfortable with your own mortality.

"DEADLY" EXPERIENCES

Are you afraid to die? I must confess that there was a time that I was afraid of death. When I was four years old, my grandfather died much too young. He was only in his late fifties. I remember seeing his body in the coffin all dressed up in blue suit and white shirt. He was going away, but I didn't understand. I just knew that it was scary to me.

Then when I was in the fourth grade, I came home from school to find my dad's car in the driveway. He was NEVER home at that time of day. Not only that, but he was not in his mechanic's clothes! He and mom told me that they had been to the doctor and my mother had tuberculosis. They explained that she would be quarantined from us for a while.

She then went away from us and spent ten months in the hospital. I couldn't see her every day. She was not there to cook for us or for me to talk with after school. I could not even get close to her for a hug. I wondered then if my mom would die. Mom didn't die. In fact, she is alive and well today, but that experience rattled my sense of security and increased my fear of death.

A couple of years later two of my friends slipped off from school at lunchtime to a home where one of them lived. There they played with a parent's loaded gun that suddenly discharged and killed one of them. I couldn't believe it! He was only 12 years old. Surely someone that young was not really gone, but I was beginning to realize that human beings are mortal.

When I was 13 years old, my favorite uncle, Bob, and his wife, Peggy, had a beautiful baby girl named Carla. My mom told me she was born with a birth defect, but that meant little to a young teen. She was so cute and cuddly, and I played with her like a toy. Then, at 17 months old, her heart suddenly stopped. At the funeral home I stared at that sweet baby girl in her tiny white coffin. She looked as if she were sleeping. I was shaken to my core. I wondered if I could die like that.

More and more I began to understand that people did not live forever. In fact, death could come suddenly... even to the very young. I knew that I did not want to die.

MY WISH TO LIVE

I want to say this loud and clear. I WANT TO LIVE A LONG TIME! I want to be 100 years old and still working, still enjoying my family, and still being active in the Lord's work. When death comes, my deep-down desire is that I will just fade away in the middle of a sermon.

Truthfully, I know that the likelihood of that is small. But no matter how long I live, I do know that my life will be too short. I know that even if I live to be 100, I will think that life has passed too fast.

Have you heard about the two turtles that collided at an intersection? The only witness to the accident was a snail. When he was interviewed about the collision, he said, *"Well... all... of... it... happened... so... fast... it... was... just... a ... blur... to... me!"*

This "speedy" accident gives me a glimpse of what will probably happen in the final moments of my life. No matter if I am 62 or 92 years, when my spirit is about to leave my body, I will probably be thinking, "It all happened so fast. It was just a big blur to me."

The great church leader James talks about this concept in his book. He said, "What is your life? It is even a vapor that appears for a little time and then vanishes away" (4:14). Our lives, mine and yours, are really just little puffs of steam. They last for a brief period and then fade away.

17

James tells us to remember that fact when we are making our plans to travel, or to make more money, or to add to our savings account. We are little puffs of steam, here right now, but gone in a little while.

CASTING OUT FEAR OF DEATH

Every one of us will die. There are no exceptions. As the Scripture tells us, "It is appointed for men to die once, but after this the judgment" (Hebrews 9:27).

As a young teenager, when I finally realized that I, too, would one day die, I feared that. Through my adult years I have witnessed many deaths, some of them significant people in my life. However, I do not fear death now.

Now, don't get me wrong. I want to live a *long* time. Not only do I want to live to be an old man, but want to live to be a *good, old* man! But here's what I mean. While I no longer fear death, I have a wife and three children who need me. I also have six grandchildren. Three of them have already lost one grandfather. I'm the only "Papaw" they have left. They need me. I want to be here for them.

If I were gone, I know that my wife, my children and my grandchildren would eventually adjust to my absence, but there are still many ways that they need me now. Heritage Christian University could find another person to take my leadership role, but there are many projects and efforts that I would leave undone. I need to finish many tasks at the university.

The apostle Paul expressed this same dilemma when he said:

"For me to live is Christ, and to die is gain. But if I

live on in the flesh, this will mean fruit from my labor; yet what I shall choose I cannot tell. For I am hard-pressed between the two, having a desire to depart and be with Christ, which is far better. Nevertheless to remain in the flesh is more needful for you" (Philippians 1:21-24).

My continued presence here on earth would allow me to make more of a difference with my life. I could see even more fruits of my labor. I could have more time to teach the gospel. I could tell more people about the great work of Heritage Christian University and encourage them to support students who serve and minister. I have a desire to do that. But even though I feel a great need to stay here on earth, I no longer fear death and departure.

Eventually, as I grew and began to study the Scriptures more, I began to understand more about this life and the life beyond. I learned a wonderful truth. Christians do not need to fear death!

Paul quotes Isaiah and Hosea in I Corinthians 15:54 and 55, "Death is swallowed up in victory. O Death, where is your sting? O Hades, where is your victory?" For the Christian, there is no sting to death. I do not have to be afraid to die. I am not going to lose the battle with death. Death cannot be victorious over me. Why? Because I am going to live forever!

You will, also. Yes, you will live forever. You will live in a different form, but you will live. The only thing that will die is your body, which is earthly and belongs here on earth. But the real you... the spirit you... will be in eternity with God. "Then the dust will return to the earth as it was, and the spirit will return to God who gave it" (Ecclesiastes 12:7).

When Christ returns, He will raise and transform our bodies to be like His own (Philippians 3:20-21). I will then live forever with Him. So death will not be victorious over the Christian. Death has no power over me and cannot sting.

But what really does sting... now remember this... what really stings is wasting your life. The sting is in living a life that just spends time, energy, and resources. It is in living a life that actually does not matter much, does not go anywhere, and does not accomplish anything worthwhile. I don't know many people who really want that kind of life, yet many are living it.

WHY THIS ELEMENT IS IMPORTANT

When you accept your own mortality and become comfortable with the idea that you will die, you then realize how short the period of time that you are allotted is. A sense of urgency begins to overtake you. You realize that you must spend your time wisely. You cannot waste it. You must live well this measured time, these few years.

Life Is Precious

Do you have a special recipe for your favorite homemade cookie? Then imagine being at work or school some morning when the craving sets in for your favorite sweet treat, those delicious cookies. All day you daydream about eating a big stack of those cookies when you get home. You know there is a fresh batch in the cookie jar. When you get home, however, you find that the "Cookie Monster" beat you there and there is only *one cookie left*!

When there is only ONE of your favorite cookies

remaining, do you gobble it down? No! You eat it slowly. You nibble at the edges. You relish every scrumptious bite. You might even lick the crumbs from your fingers. You savor the taste, making it last as long as you can.

That's the way your *life* must be lived. You have only one life. It is precious and priceless. You cannot waste it. Savor it! Enjoy it! Make the most of it! And make it last as long as you can.

To do that means you must have your priorities in order. You must get done the most important things. You no longer have time to waste on trivial matters.

Your actions must be appropriate. Being angry over a minor event is no longer important. The lack of a promotion at work does not have the power to upset your day or your life as it did before.

When life is precious, your decisions must reflect integrity of spirit. You make decisions based on the moral beliefs which have molded your heart.

Your behavior must reflect congruency of heart and hand. The love, joy, goodness, and gentleness of your life must be the outward signs of your own inward peace. When these things are evident in your life, you are indicating that you realize life is precious and that you will treasure it.

Accept the fact that you are mortal and your time is short. Only then are you on the road to making your life count.

One Chance to Give

I've only got one life to live
One chance to give.
One time to make it count
And time does not stand still.
I've only got one life to share
To show that Jesus cares.
And to do the Lord's will
I've only got one life to live.
It seems like yesterday
when I was just a boy
And I wasted so much time
that I missed the joy.
But Jesus forgave my sins
He remembers no more.
And the rest of my life
I'll live just for the Lord.
I've only got one life to live
One chance to give.

--Carroll Robinson

2 Corinthians 5:17

Therefore, if anyone is in Christ, he is a new creation; old things have passed away; behold, all things have become new.

In the next few pages you will discover that:

* ❖ Knowing God's word is the first step to being a new person.
* ❖ By changing yourself, you will set off an immeasurable chain of influence.
* ❖ You will change the world if you care.

Principle Three

⯎⯎Determine to Change the World⯎⯎

> As a salesman drove into a small southern town, he saw an old man seated on a bench in the town square, whittling and enjoying the sunshine. Pulling up to the curb for directions, the salesman leaned out his window. Wishing to make conversation, he said, "Hey, old timer, you lived her all your life?"
>
> The old man slowly raised his head, looked the salesman in the eye, and dryly said, "Not yet!"

Just like that old man, you have not yet lived the rest of your life. The important question then remains: What will you do with the life you have left? Will you drift through each day without a purpose? Will you give your all to work, to pleasure, or to the pursuit of money or power? The way you decide what to do with the life you have left will determine whether your life has meaning.

If you want your life to make a difference, you can only answer the question of what you will do with the life you have left in one way. That is the third important element of making your life count: *Determine to change the world with the time you have here.*

CHANGING THE WORLD

If you determine to change the world with the rest of

your life, a logical question may occur to you: How *do* I change the world?

I want to suggest two things in answer to that. These two things are not profound or even original. They are the simplest reduction of numerous theories of change, but they are the building stones for changing the world.

The number one way to change the world is to *change yourself first*. See, I told you it was simple–in principle, at least. The difficulty comes in doing it.

The Christian life is all about change. When a person becomes a Christian, that person's life begins to change. When someone obeys God and passes from being lost to being saved, the Spirit of God changes his perspective on everything– family, church, work, recreation, conversation, and leisure time. No longer does he look at family as a burden or as an entity to serve him. Work is no longer the major focus of life, nor is it even a series of tasks to slog through until the weekend. The predominant purpose in his life is no longer planning how he will spend his leisure time or how he will get ahead at work.

Everything changes when a person becomes a "new creation" in Christ. "Therefore, if anyone is in Christ, he is a new creation; old things have passed away; behold, all things have become new" (2 Corinthians 5:17).

Now, you may be thinking, "Well, my life didn't change all that much when I became a Christian." If your life has not changed, then it may be time to consider whether you have allowed Christ to be the Lord of your life. Have you permitted God to begin shaping and molding your heart through the teaching of His Word? Have you allowed Him to change your heart as you do His Will? If the honest answer is "no" or "not really", then you need to take that first step immediately. Get to know God and His perspective. Practice the principles that you read and learn from His Word.

Unless you become a Christian and allow God to change you, you cannot hope to change the world in a positive way. If, however, you allow God to be in charge of your life, you will begin a process that will automatically result in change. Let's read that last sentence again. You will begin a process that will automatically result in change.

Here's the way the process works. If God becomes Lord of your life, you will begin to want to know more about Him. That means you will begin to study His Word more.

Step 1: You begin to know God through His Word.

When you begin to immerse yourself in God's Word, the Word begins to be your new standard of behavior. Because it is a new standard, your behavior will begin to change to fit the new standard. You will begin to conform more and more to the model you see in the Scriptures.

Step 2: The Word develops a new standard of behavior for you.

As you work to do His Will more often, the truth and the benefits of His commandments will be more apparent to you. As they are, your faith in God builds. You begin to take on a new attitude, the attitude of Christ.

Step 3: Realizing the truth of God's commands builds your faith.

Day by day, as you live for Him, God begins to shape your heart and mind. Things that

Step 4: God begins to shape your heart and mind.

once appealed to you have no more attraction. Behaviors that were once detrimental to you and to others begin to be replaced by positive, beneficial actions.

The changes in your life will soon become apparent to others. You begin to change and be shaped by your new behaviors.

> *Step 5: Your new behaviors and attitude begin to change your relationships.*

All of these changes result from allowing God to be in charge of your life. As soon as you determine to be obedient to Him and allow Him to be Lord of your life, you have taken the first step toward changing yourself.

When that happens, you will notice something amazing. Your world will begin to change. That change occurs because you, as a changed person, begin to interact with others differently. By changing the way you interact with other people, you change their actions with you. That change begins to influence the entire interaction of humanity, which eventually changes the world.

So, not only does *your* world change, but *the* world begins to change. The little sphere that you live and work in daily changes dramatically with your new perspective, attitude, and behaviors. Beyond that, however, the world begins to change. Let me give you an example of what I mean.

Counselors at the Alpha Center, located on the campus of HCU, tell me that many married couples in distress think that nothing will change in their marriage unless they both work diligently to improve their marriage. While that is the ideal situation, the reality is that one partner might be able to bring about tremendous change in the marriage by working alone. That change begins with the individual working to change self.

Newly married couples speak to each other, react to each other, and behave toward each other in ways that begin to develop patterns over the years of their marriage. Sometimes, without love and respect, those patterns become destructive.

When a husband or wife realizes that their pattern of interaction is harmful to the marriage, that individual can determine to change his or her own reactions, words, or behaviors. That spouse can begin to reflect respect, admiration, and love. She can decide to speak with kindness and consideration. A husband can decide to care for his wife with loving behaviors.

When that happens, the other spouse often begins to relate differently, and the marriage changes for the better. When the couple improves their marriage, they influence their children, their community, and their church in a more positive way. The influence of a single individual who changes self cannot be measured.

The Butterfly Effect

One individual who determines to make one positive change in himself can set off a chain reaction of influence that is immeasurable. This type of influence is much like the Butterfly Effect, first named in the 1960s by Edward Lorenz.

Lorenz, a meteorologist, was running computerized equations to predict the weather. He ran one equation and got a response. The next time he rounded the initial number, which was only an infinitesimal change. He expected to have a similar result.

Lorenz discovered, however, that even the slightest difference in the initial condition, even a rounded number, could make prediction impossible. After extensive research and trials, he made a presentation of his findings. He titled his talk, "Does the Flap of a Butterfly's Wings in Brazil Set Off a Tornado in Texas?"

That the quiet flap of a butterfly's wing could influence such a distant and destructive event as a tornado in Texas boggles my mind. However, small actions have the capacity to create other actions, even years later, of tornadic proportions.

A teacher who decides to treat a troublesome student with caring encouragement can trigger a series of reactions that change that student's life forever. A woman, estranged from her sister for years, who decides to reach out in love and concern can change that relationship and all the peripheral relationships in an entire family.

Any small action, whether positive or destructive, sets in motion a chain of events that can change the world for worse or for better. And, as Lorenz indicated, such a slight change makes predictability impossible. We may never know on this side of eternity the tremendous influence of any one of our actions.

Individual Power

About this time, you may be thinking: "My world is relatively small. I'm a quiet person with just a few close friends and a small family. I don't have much power or influence. Surely, my actions do not have the capacity to change much of anything."

I would ask that you reconsider your individual

power. My favorite definition of "power" is this: *The ability to influence the thinking and action of others.* Most of us probably think that we do not have much power. Yet experts tell us that the average person directly influences at least 250 people in a normal life span.

Having direct influence over 250 people is quite powerful. But here is what is exciting– *Christians are not average people!* They seriously work at changing the lives of others in positive ways. I believe that Christians have the opportunity to influence directly, not just 250 others, but thousands of people.

Christians make deliberate efforts to teach and to serve in various ways. They support mission efforts, they serve food to the homeless, they repair homes for the elderly, and they care for abandoned and neglected children. When they do, they influence hundreds and hundreds of people. By their influence over those people, they change the world.

Now that is real power! Changing yourself is the first step toward changing the world.

CARING

The second step toward changing the world is to *care*. I once heard an on-the-street interview conducted with a 10-year-old boy. The interviewer was promoting a foundation that worked with inner city schools to develop leadership in children. He asked the boy, "What is leadership?" and stuck the microphone under his chin. The kid blinked, looked to the side for a couple of seconds, and then uttered one of the most profound statements about leadership I have ever heard!

He turned to face the camera and said, "Leadership is making a difference. And to make a difference, all you have to do is care." Wow! That kid is on to something.

If you want to make a difference in the world, you must care. People who care cannot stay idle and allow the world to deteriorate around them. They must do something.

If you care, then you will work to improve a situation, rescue a person, or repair a relationship. You will not be able to see a child in neglect or a family in danger without giving of yourself or your means. You will not stand idly by while a friend self-destructs with an addiction. You will not be able to keep from helping the poor, the sick, the widowed, or the orphaned. You will do something to improve their situations. You are wired to do something because you care.

Caring means you will respond to a neighbor when a family member is hospitalized. You will provide comfort when a friend loses a spouse to death. You will gather clothes and food when fire destroys a home. You will take a neglected child under your wing. You will traipse through mud and debris to rebuild a home for a hurricane victim. You will offer counsel and wisdom to a couple who struggle with their marriage.

Each time you care enough to serve, you change a life for the better. Each time you influence a life in a positive way you begin to change the world. Change yourself first, and then care enough to reach out to others.

THE WORLD WILL BE BETTER

Do you remember the old song, *The Impossible Dream*? One of the verses begins like this:

To be willing to give
When there's nothing to give

And to be willing to die
So that honor and justice may live
And I know if I'll be true to this glorious quest
That my heart will lie peaceful and calm
When I'm laid to my rest
And the world will be better for this.

(Lyrics, Mitch Leigh; Music, Joe Darion, Cherry Lane Music)

The last three lines of that song are special to me. Notice these two lines: *That my heart will lie peaceful and calm when I'm laid to my rest.* How do you leave this earth and go to the other side with a calm and peaceful heart?

You cannot go calmly unless you have been redeemed by the Savior and your sins have been forgiven. Beyond that, however, your heart will lie peaceful only if you have made your life count.

And the world will be better for this. You need to know for sure that your life has made the world better. When you are nearing your life's end, there will be nothing like the sweet satisfaction you feel knowing that the world is a better place because you have lived in it.

Change the world by changing yourself first, and then make a difference by letting your caring, loving life touch others. When you do, you can leave this earth knowing that you have made your life count.

Proverbs 4:23

Keep your heart with all diligence, for out of it spring the issues of life.

In the next few pages you will discover that:

- ❖ You gain control by surrendering your uncontrollable problems to God.

- ❖ You must take responsibility for controlling what is within your power to do so.

Principle Four

ॐ☙Take Responsibility for Your Life☙ॐ

In *The Seven Habits of Highly Effective People*, Stephen Covey asks his readers to imagine their own funeral. Four speakers at each funeral are the reader's spouse, neighbor, best friend, and co-worker. Then Covey asks readers to imagine what each person will say. What a powerful and transforming image!

What will people say at your funeral? Their eulogies will reflect how you have lived your life. If you want the speakers to talk about your good influence on others, then live in such a way that you influence other people for good. If you want them to talk of your service to the community, then put yourself in positions where you can serve others.

If you want the eulogies at your funeral to talk of your devotion to your God, then live that way now. The difference you can make in the world is dependent on what you are doing *now* to influence others positively, to serve unselfishly, and to love and fear God.

What you do today and tomorrow and the next day will determine the meaning of your life. If you truly want to make your life count, *take personal responsibility for the way you are living your life now.*

If you take an honest look at your life now and decide that it is not as "pretty" as it needs to be, take responsibility for that. Admit your weaknesses, do something about correcting them, and then manage the direction of the rest of your life.

If you want your life to count, first of all make sure that it is pointed in the direction God would have it go. Then work at living each day so that in your twilight years just before you pass to the other side, you will have satisfaction of knowing your life has meant something to the world.

SURRENDER

Taking full responsibility for your life does not mean that you will be able to control everything that happens to you. Many things in life are simply out of your personal control. Did you ever try to stop a hurricane? How about a tornado? Of course not. Those things cannot be controlled by humans.

No one can control sudden losses. You cannot control the loss of a loved one, the closing of the company where you have worked for years, the loss of your house by fire or tornado, the death of a child through that child's self-destructive decisions, or the loss of health by a devastating auto accident caused by a drunken driver. All of these and numerous other circumstances are beyond your power, energy, or strength to control.

In fact, some things are just too big for any *person*. They are so big that friends and contacts can't help. Education, money, and knowledge are useless. Neither the government nor any other entity will be able to keep you from some of life's problematic events.

So, how do you take responsibility when things are beyond your control? The answer is simple. You don't even try. You surrender!

Now, don't get me wrong. Surrender is not giving yourself over to the enemy who has defeated you. Surrender is not folding your hands as you sigh and say, "I give up."

The kind of surrender that I am writing about involves giving over all those bigger-than-you-are problems to the One who can handle them. Surrender in that case is taking that out-of-control issue and laying it at the Lord's feet. When you do, you say, "Lord, this is too big for me. I can't handle it, and so I am surrendering it to you." Then you give it over to Him and trust that He will help you through.

When you surrender your heavy burdens to the One who can carry them, you can have confidence that no burden will be able to defeat you. In fact, not only will you not be defeated, but you will always come out the decisive victor.

Taking responsibility for your life means realizing that some things are simply too much to handle and control. When that happens, give them over. Then you no longer need to fret and stew over those things. You won't need to wake up at 2:00 a.m. trying to work out solutions. You won't even need to try to manipulate circumstances or people to gain relief from pain. You just simply surrender.

CONTROL

Surrendering, however, is only a part of taking responsibility. The other part of that is *control*. Sounds like a contradiction, doesn't it? But it isn't.

Be responsible for surrendering the things that are beyond your control, but take responsibility for controlling the things that are within your power to do so. A hurricane and a spouse's death are uncontrollable events in our lives that need to be surrendered. But many other occurrences, decisions, and actions are within your control.

God has given you a brain and abilities. He expects you to use them to make effective decisions and to seize opportunities. He has given you freedom of will and choice. Because of that He will not take control away from you in some facets of your life.

The following are four areas of life that God allows you to control:

1. Your *behavior.*

God does not force you to behave in any certain way. In effect He says, "You control your behavior. That's within your power." Where you go, what you say, and what you do are under your own control. He allows you the freedom to blow up in anger or to speak kind words and to behave with grace and dignity or to act like a jerk. You can be disrespectful to the elderly or tenderly care for your grandparents. If you choose, you can act selfishly or you can give yourself in service to others.

The way you behave is entirely within your control. The responsibility for your behavior rests on your shoulders only. Blaming other people or circumstances will not work. When you stop shifting responsibility for your actions and assume the full burden, you are moving toward being in control.

2. Your *attitude.*

Your attitude comes from your expectations, which come from your belief system. Your belief system is whatever you have programmed into your heart. And, after you become an adult, you have control over the programming.

Consider Proverbs 4:23, "Keep your heart with all diligence, for out of it spring the issues of life." Note Ephesians 4:23, "Be renewed in the spirit (attitude) of your mind." Romans 12:2 indicates, "Do not be conformed to this world, but be transformed by the renewing of your mind..."

Good people treasure good in their hearts. They think good thoughts. They feed their minds with good things. They continually seek to improve the mind and spirit.

Evil people are evil because they "store up" evil in their hearts (Luke 6:45). They think bad thoughts. They feed their minds with corrupt and evil words and images. They are not interested in improving but only in satisfying their insatiable desires to do evil.

You have direct control over what you put into your heart... what you read, what you hear, what movies, TV shows and online sites you watch, and what you meditate upon. All of these feed your belief system, set up your expectations, and affect your attitude.

Guard your heart by making sure you nurture it with good things. Feed your mind with things that are noble, trustworthy, and excellent. You have direct control over that.

3. Your *goals*.

Goals are simply dreams with a deadline. Your dreams pull you forward into the future, but the Lord doesn't dream your dreams for you. You set your own aspirations and goals. You have control over the things you work to achieve. You can work for material possessions, status, or power, or you can work to pursue the image of Christ.

You can set goals that can help you achieve success, as the world defines success. You can set out to become the top in your profession. You may become the president of your own company. You can choose to pursue money, and you may become one of the world's wealthiest people. You can even set a goal to become a great political leader. Since goal setting is a powerful instrument to help you achieve, you may reach any of those goals.

Not one of those goals is a bad one. In fact, many Christians have risen to the top of their professions, many have attained wealth, and many have become leaders in the political arena. But overarching any of those goals is the one that is far superior and more long lasting. The goal of becoming more like Christ allows you to have a meaningful life, whether or not you achieve any of the other things.

You get to choose your goals. You have complete freedom to decide which ones you give your life to achieve.

4. Your *decisions*.

You have control over the choices you make. When you go to a cafeteria for dinner, God doesn't make you choose the gooey chocolate cheesecake over the no-fat, no-sugar gelatin dessert. You have a choice. While that decision may make little difference in your life (other than a few pounds if you decide to eat cheesecake regularly!), there are three choices that make a huge difference in how your life goes. You have control over these three choices.

Consider the following:

• *Who you live your life WITH.*

I heard once about a lady who wore her wedding ring on her index finger instead of her left ring finger. Someone asked her, "Do you realize you have your wedding band on the wrong finger?"

She replied, "I married the wrong man!"

The woman's reply brings a chuckle, but the truth is the decision about who you marry is your choice. In essence, the Lord says, "I trust you to use the brain I gave you, to be discerning, and to make a wise decision about your choice of a life's companion."

The one decision about who will be your life's mate has led many people to heaven and others to a hell on earth. There are many spouses who are converted to Christ because of their Christian mates. Others are dissuaded from having anything to do with church or Christian friends.

Some spouses encourage their mates daily to lead better lives. Others create havoc in their families and keep their mates in turmoil. The decision about your mate is within your control. Be sure it is a wise one.

• *What you live your life DOING.*

Whatever you choose as your life's work is your decision. God has given you specific abilities that can lead you in particular directions. Assess those abilities, carefully evaluate the choices, and select the one that will help you live close to God, have adequate time for family, and give you a sense of accomplishment. That is your choice.

Some people have allowed money or prestige to guide their choice of career. Others have been lured by fame and status. Because of their choices of the type of work they do, some people have lost their families and forsaken their God.

I once watched a TV movie, the title of which I never knew. The leading male character was a member of Congress who had set an early goal to achieve money and power. He was attracted to a young female lawyer who had become a consumer advocate.

Over dinner one day, he questioned her about the reasons she didn't use her professional credentials and abilities to make a lot of money. She obviously had considerable talent and education.

Her answer was interesting. She told him, "I've been in that world, but I made a change."

When he asked why she had made a change, she quietly said, "My life must have meaning."

While I certainly do not believe a person must be poor and work at an unskilled job to have a meaningful life, the woman's words are worth reflection. The pursuit of money, status, and prestige did not bring meaning to her life. By themselves, those goals could not give her a sense of purpose and satisfaction. Working for something larger than herself gave her a sense of fulfillment.

Your selection of your life's work is within your control. Choose wisely and enjoy your work and your life.

• *Who you live your life FOR.*

You have three choices in this area. You can choose to try *to live up to others' expectations.* If you do, you will always feel jerked this way and that. You may even feel that you have a ball and chain or that you are boxed in. You can never live up to everybody's expectations of you.

You can also decide *to live your life for yourself*. If you choose to do so, you will have a friendship-starved life and die a lonely death. Human beings were never created to live in isolation but to live in a network of relationships.

We are born dependent on our mothers and fathers. When we leave our parents' care and become "independent", we quickly realize that happiness comes, not from independence, but from relating with others–a mate, friends, and close associates. Humans are created to grow and develop within a network of interdependent relationships.

So those two choices will not bring satisfaction throughout life. The only choice that brings satisfaction is deciding *to live for the Lord*. Anyone, including self, who is above the Lord in your life is going to cause you trouble.

When you live to please God, however, you automatically look out for the best interests of self and others. Why? Because He teaches you how to love. He teaches you how to have a sincere desire for the welfare and best interests of others. He teaches you how to care for yourself and love others accordingly. Prioritizing so that God is first will bring a peaceful heart.

Take personal responsibility for your behavior, your thoughts and attitudes, your goals and decisions, and your choices about a mate, a career, and the one who has top priority in your life. Those things are within your power to control. Be responsible for controlling them.

John 18:37

For this cause I was born, and for this cause I have come into the world, that I should bear witness to the truth.

In the next few pages you will discover that:

- ❖ You have an individual purpose in life.
- ❖ Your purpose will control your life.
- ❖ Your controlled life will result in three changes.

Principle Five

☙❧Have a Sense of Purpose❧☙

> A TV interviewer once asked
> General Norman Schwarzkopf to explain
> the difference between the decisive quick
> victory in Desert Storm and the
> quagmire of Vietnam.
> He replied, "In Vietnam, we did
> not understand why we were there. But
> in Desert Storm, we knew we were there
> to get the Iraqis out of Kuwait. People
> can do amazing things when they know
> what their purpose is."

Just as an army must know its purpose in order to fight its enemies most effectively, so do we function better and accomplish more when we have a sense of purpose. Jesus is the perfect illustration of a life that was purpose-centered. Pontius Pilate once asked Jesus, "Are you the king of the Jews?" Jesus calmly replied, "For this cause I was born, and for this cause I have come into the world..." (John 18:37). Jesus knew clearly what His purpose was, and in three short years, He amazingly transformed the world.

Our God is a God of purpose. Notice these words in Paul's letter to the Ephesians: "Just as He chose us in Him before the foundation of the world" (1:4), "having made known to us the mystery of His will, according to His good pleasure which He purposed in Himself (1:9), and "according to the eternal *purpose* which He accomplished in Christ Jesus our Lord" (3:11).

Because we are made in His image, then it rightly follows that He also designed us to be people of purpose. If you want to do amazing things with your life, you must *have a sense of purpose.*

YOUR PURPOSE

At some point or other, almost everyone wonders, "Why am I here? Why was I born?" Have you considered what your purpose is?

I cannot tell you what your own personal purpose is. What I can tell you is that you are not here by accident. You are here because God allowed you to be conceived and born with His Spirit within. God has no accidental births. You were born, as you are, for a reason.

Although I don't know what your individual purpose is, the Scriptures give us a clear picture and guidance about what God's purpose is for all Christians. In John 6, a ragtag crowd of people who had been waiting for Jesus on the far side of the Galilee Sea searched for Him on the other side. They had been begging for and searching for relief from their suffering lives. Aimless and concerned with the physical aspect of living, they clamored for His attention.

Seeking some answers, they came to the only one who held promise of relief. He quickly pointed out that they were seeking Him only because He had fed loaves and fishes to the crowd on the Tiberian side of Galilee. He urged them to be more concerned with their spiritual and eternal needs.

They then asked what they had to do to work the works of God. In other words, what are we supposed to do with our lives if we follow God? How do we know that we are doing what He intended? How do we make our lives count for Him? Those are the questions that each one of us is still asking today.

So what did Jesus answer? He replied, "This is the work of God, that you believe in Him whom He sent" (verse 29). He turned their attention entirely away from their physical needs and pointed them to the living water and the bread of life.

Belief in Jesus! What a purpose for life!

That scripture indicates that the purpose of your life, and mine, is to believe that Jesus Christ is God's Son. He was sent to rescue you and me from sin. He lived a perfect life and shed His innocent blood so we could be forgiven. Because of our lack of perfection, we can't pay the penalty for our sins and be reconciled to God. Jesus paid that penalty for us.

Can you believe that with all your heart? If so, then you are on the path to knowing what your individual purpose is.

Without this belief and the obedience that must accompany it, your life will be wasted. You may make millions of dollars. You may even have a doctoral degree from the finest university in the world. You may be the most popular person in your community. You may hold the highest office in the land, but if you do not believe and obey Jesus Christ, then your life will always be off kilter. It will never make sense.

PURPOSE LEADS TO CONTROL

Having a sense of purpose controls your life. Jesus often made statements like, "I came from heaven to..." or, "For this purpose I came," He knew why His Father had sent Him. He knew why He had left heaven. He had a strong sense of purpose, and that purpose controlled everything He did in the short time He was here. He did not get sidetracked with anything that was not related to His purpose.

If you have a mission, then living is simpler. Decisions are easier to make. When you face a dilemma, you can look at your choices and ask, "Does this choice or the other help me attain my purpose?" Then you can choose the one that helps you to accomplish your mission.

Where you live, what you do for a living, whom you marry and choose for friends, and how you spend your leisure time are decisions that become simpler if a sense of purpose guides them.

If you are a person of purpose faced with a decision about a new job, you will ask, "Will this job help me to accomplish my purpose?" If you are purposeful and you fall in love and are considering marriage, you will ask, "Will this person be a help or a hindrance to my purpose?"

Even if you occasionally get off track, you can always find the right path if you remember your purpose... if you remember where you were going when you strayed.

THE NEXT STEP

So let us say that you believe in Jesus with all your heart and you have followed the steps that lead you to be *in* Christ. The question you may have now is, "Where do I go

48

from here?" What happens next, and how do you find your individual purpose?

I can't tell you exactly what will happen in your own life, but I can tell you what results from having a purpose. If you center your life on your belief in Jesus, you will begin to notice three changes in your life:

❖ *Spiritual growth.*

If you truly believe that He is the Son of God and that your purpose is to honor and please Him, then you will naturally seek to know more about Him. You will start working on finding out everything you can about Him.

You will read the Bible because you want to know more about this God and His Son in whom you believe. You will begin to think more about Jesus, His commands, and His life. You may even begin to read spiritual, inspiring books, and attend lectureships and workshops.

The Heritage Christian University Annual Evangelism Workshop, held each year the last full week in September, is filled with attendees who can't get enough of the excellent teaching and encouragement that are always present.

You will begin to pray more. You may feel awkward initially, but over time, prayer will become a habit. You will not use prayer any longer just when you need something. You will praise Him more and thank Him more often. You may even begin to include the needs of others when you pray. As time goes by, your prayers will become more personal as God becomes more real.

Meanwhile, your knowledge of God is growing and you are beginning to understand His absolute love and care for you. You are beginning to realize that His commands are always for our benefit. With this kind of realization, you begin to concentrate on right living, on controlling self, on caring for your brothers and sisters, and on meditating about things that are noble, pure, and praiseworthy.

With right living, control, care, and meditation your character begins to transform itself. You begin to grow spiritually. You become more and more like the Son that you have read and studied about.

When you begin to do all these things, then, spiritually, you grow by leaps and bounds. The growth is a natural result of your belief in Jesus Christ.

Life is about spiritual growth. It is not about feeding your family. It is not about working for awards and achievements. Life is about growing spiritually.

❖ *Learning to Love.*

The next change you will notice is that you will begin to love more because spiritual growth is about love. Love is a natural result if you are working to become more godly. As you begin to know God, who is love (I John 4:8), and begin to be transformed into the image of His Son, the natural result is that you will learn to love.

The world rattles off the word *love* as freely as water flows in a stream. We say that we love hot dogs or strawberry shortcake. A woman may say she loves the red dress in the department store window or the strappy high heels her friend is wearing. A man may mention how he loves his truck or his favorite meal.

What we usually mean by that is that we have an intense *liking* for a particular object. That is not love.

Real love is sometimes hard work. The real love that

is hard work is not the mushy, head-over-heels kind of love. It's not even the love you have for your children, parents, your mate or best friends. That kind of love is usually easy. Jesus said that even sinners can love like that (Luke 6:32). He is calling on you and me to rise above the normal and natural and do the hard work of love.

The hard work kind of love is the kind that loves your enemy and those who persecute you or talk negatively about you. It loves those who may be difficult to love. It loves those who push you away. It loves those who are in need– the poor, the sick, the addicted, and the sinners.

Real love is not always convenient, not always clean, and not always conscious of time or obligations. It is not easy, but it is a natural result of your spiritual growth.

❖ *Making a difference.*

Learning to love is the process of making a difference with your life. When you acquire real love, it will compel you to make a difference. If you love, you will not be able to stand by and simply watch while people suffer or their lives fall apart. If you love, you will be concerned about the welfare of your church, your family, your business, your job, your community. You will feel compelled to do something to make a difference.

When a neighbor is hurting because her husband left her for another woman, love pulls you to be there for her. When a child is abused, your love compels you to take action.

When an acquaintance is desperately sick in the hospital, love pushes you to make sure his family's needs are addressed. When a missionary tells you of an urgent need, your love for the lost causes you to reach for your wallet. It may even compel you to determine that you will give your vacation time next summer to helping.

Having a purpose means you will grow spiritually because you want to be more like Jesus. When you grow spiritually, then you will learn to love. When you learn to love and do the hard work of love, you will feel compelled to make a difference. It all ties together.

FROM PURPOSE TO GROWTH

Having a purpose and a complete belief in Jesus will naturally lead you to control your life. With a strong faith and a controlled life, you will begin to grow spiritually.

When your spiritual life expands, you will learn to love. It's a natural outgrowth of focusing on God, who is synonymous with love.

Love, then, will push you to be fully engaged with all kinds of people and circumstances. Love will cause you to get your hands dirty and to give of yourself, even when it is inconvenient. You will care for the needy. You will befriend the lonely widow. You will feed the homeless. You will tend the sick. You will teach the lost.

That kind of compelling love is the kind God has.

"For God so loved the world, that He gave His only begotten Son..." (John 3:16). He loved us so much that He couldn't help but give that which was most precious to Him.

Real love will make you do things you wouldn't ordinarily do. And that is when amazing things begin to happen. Your world begins to change. The world begins to change.

Have a sense of purpose. It will change your life.

Romans 12:6

Having then gifts differing according to the grace that is given to us, let us use them...

In the next few pages you will discover that:

❖ You have gifts different from others because of your gender, your personality, and your culture.

❖ Whatever your gifts are, they are to be used in the service of God.

❖ You may find your gifts by what others tell you or do not tell you.

Principle Six

৯৯Find and Develop Your Gift৶৶

> *A friend of mine who preaches in Florida recently told me about the growth his church is experiencing. I asked how he had been able to accomplish that.*
>
> *Pausing for a moment, he said, "I'm not sure it has anything to do with me or my preaching."*
>
> *He went on to explain, "We have an elder who teaches an adult class. Visitors come from all over to hear him teach the Scriptures. I've never seen anyone who can make Scripture come alive like he does. He helps people see how it applies to their lives."*
>
> *He smiled and commented with admiration, "He is simply gifted as a teacher."*

What a joy to be a student in that elder's class! To hear the Word of God fly off the page and into the heart, to have the imagination engaged by carefully chosen words, and to see the connection between problems in daily life and solutions in the Scriptures...what abundant blessings! That church leader is enriching the lives of every student by using the special gift God has given him.

To find meaning in your own life and to make a difference in others' lives, *find and develop your gift.*

55

Perhaps you are even multi-gifted and display ability in several life areas. When used, each of them will enrich your life and make it count.

DIFFERENCES

Before we can discuss your particular gift (or gifts, as they may be), we need to make one point crystal clear. This will not be a revelation to you. We all understand it, but our actions tell us, particularly in the church, that this is something we frequently forget. Here is the point: *People are different.*

Did you get that? People are *different.*

Not only are they different, but they are exceedingly different. The differences are most obvious in four essential areas.

Gender Differences

For years, some sociologists and feminists tried to promote the idea that men and women are different only because they are socialized to be so. But in the last several years research has confirmed what God's people have always known. Men and women are physically and emotionally wired *differently.*

They do not think the same. They do not react in the same way. Their emotions may not even be similar. If husbands and wives do not know this instinctively, a few short years of marriage will let them know with certainty just how different they are!

When a husband comes home, frustrated and troubled over something that happened at work, his wife may beg him to tell her about it. But all he wants to do is to putter in his workshop or lie in the recliner and think about the problem. He may need to ponder it long enough for it to make sense and for him to construct a solution.

When he has done that, he may tell his wife the whole story and what he is going to do about it. Or... he may not.

On the other hand, if his wife is having a disagreement with her son's teacher, she wants something entirely different. She will tell her best friend, her mother, her sister, and maybe even the grocery clerk. She will most certainly want to tell her husband about every word that was said, where it occurred, who else was there, and how everybody else reacted. In fact, while she is talking, her husband may be thinking that surely she has used up her daily quota of words by now!

When she finally winds down, if her husband's first words are, "Well, this is what you should do...," he has totally turned her off. She does not want him to solve her problem; she only wants him to listen.

In general, men take a straight-line approach. They think (a) Here's a problem, (b) I will ruminate on it by myself, and (c) I will solve it. While a and c are the same for women, b (the route to the solution) is completely different. The route to solving the problem for women may be to discuss it with others and get their ideas. Neither the straight-line approach nor the open discussion is the *right* way. They are just different.

Cultural Differences

People are also different because of the culture in which they live. Each semester the campus at HCU is filled with students from about 12 to 16 different cultures.

When students from India, Jamaica, Peru, Mexico,

Zimbabwe, Scotland, Liberia, England, Samoa, St. Vincent, Romania, Honduras, Australia, Switzerland, Ghana, South Africa, and the United States live and work together, they learn more than we can ever teach them in a classroom.

One of the worst things we could do is try to convert those wonderful students to the American culture.

We have laughed together at their stories of trying to understand the speech of the Deep South. We have learned together how to share the gospel without offense in a culture different from ours. We have introduced each other to customs that seem strange or awkward. We have also learned what nonverbal behaviors *not* to use.

In some Asian countries, for example, we have learned that crossing one's legs so that the bottom of the shoe is seen is considered offensive. We have learned that in some parts of the world, bringing the thumb and forefinger together to make the OK sign is considered a vulgar gesture. How different we all are! And yet we have benefited from the richness of these experiences of differences.

Personality Differences

People are also different from each other because of their unique personalities. No one is a carbon copy of someone else. Just like snowflakes, each one of us has a unique imprint. Some people are quiet and reserved; others are outgoing and flamboyant. Some folks never meet a stranger, while others take hours to warm up to a new acquaintance. We all have quirks of personality that distinguish us from everybody else. Your individual personality is your own, and so is mine.

Differences in Gifts

These differences in gender, culture, and personality

mean that God has created each person in a unique form. Each one of us has abilities that are different from everybody else, and they equip us to do different things in life.

Chapter 12 of Romans lists several different gifts that God has given to individuals to be used in His service– prophecy, ministry, teaching, exhortation, giving, leading, and the showing of mercy.

Notice, however, that this list of gifts is prefaced with a caution. The author Paul notes in verse 3 that no one should "think of himself more highly than he ought to think, but to think soberly, as God has dealt to each one a measure of faith." Having a special gift does not give you a reason to be conceited or to think that you are special just because God has given you a special gift. God does not love you more because He gave you a gift that He did not give your friend or neighbor. He has simply equipped each of you with different gifts.

Does God love us all? Yes! Did He create us all equal? No, we are equal only in value. Some of you are stronger than I am. Many (most?) of you are more intelligent than I. You can run faster than I can. You can talk more effectively than I can, or organize better, or comfort more. God does love us all the same, but we are not all equal in abilities.

GIFTS

❖ Prophecy

The list of abilities beginning in verse 6 is only a list of *types* of gifts God gives. This is not meant to be an exhaustive list.

The list begins with prophecy. The modern-day equivalent is preaching. God never intended for everyone to preach. What a madhouse the church would become on Sundays if all the men decided to preach! But some people are gifted in that area.

Frequently I have doubted whether that is one of my gifts. On many Sunday nights I have almost decided to quit preaching!

When I first began as a young preacher, I had one sermon on world evangelism I had preached several times. I knew that sermon well. After all, it had only three points.

One night I was invited to preach to a church in Sheffield, Alabama. The building was packed. I began my sermon and, being full of knowledge (and of myself), I was soon on my second point. My youthful zeal took over and I began gesturing enthusiastically, so much so that I knocked my outline and all my notes right off the pulpit. They sailed out into space and landed under the front pew.

I hesitated only a moment while thinking, "No problem. I know this sermon. I just have one more point anyway." So I completed the second point and said, "And my third point is..."

There was dead silence. The computer in my brain had just crashed. No matter how many times I hit the restart button, there was no third point anywhere in my head.

After what must have been the longest 10 seconds in history, I quickly said, "And I will tell you that third point as soon as I get my notes." I stumbled down the steps, retrieved the papers, and lamely finished the sermon, which as I reflect on it now, was not very good anyway.

I'm still preaching, but do I have the gift of

preaching? I don't know. Some people have it, and what a joy it is to listen. But not everyone can expect to be gifted like that.

❖ Ministry

Ministry simply means service. Although all Christians are to be ministers, or servants, some have a special gift for service. They seem to know what to do, they know how to do it, and they know when it's appropriate.

When someone is sick, that gifted person knows exactly what the sick one needs. If it is water, if it is a cool cloth, if it is taking care of a worry about their children or the household chores, the gifted one seems to know it instinctively.

There was a death recently in our congregation. When I visited the family, I was astounded to discover that two gifted servants had appeared at their doorstep early that morning and left enough paper plates, cups, napkins, and breakfast food for the many extended family members who had quickly gathered at the news of the death. The family was so grateful for that quiet, thoughtful gift. That was one worry off their shoulders.

Doing something like that never occurred to me. But it seems natural to someone who has the gift of service.

❖ Teaching

This chapter began with the story of someone who has a special gift for teaching. Those of us who have sat at the feet of a truly gifted teacher realize the difference.

If you want to see misery personified, check out the students in a Bible class taught by someone who has no gift for teaching. This one is yawning, that one has her head on the desk, another is passing notes, and the eyes of the others are glazed. There just seems to be little connection between the teacher and the hearts of the students.

Oh, but let a gifted teacher take the same class of students and look at the excitement! One raises her hand to ask a question, two or three others are eager to answer the interesting question posed by the teacher, and another asks to meet the teacher after class for more discussion.

How much better it is to have fewer classes with better teachers than to have a large number of classes taught by boring, half-interested teachers. A gifted teacher can make the Word of God what it truly is–exciting and interesting, capturing our thoughts and hearts.

❖ Exhortation

I call this gift coaching. It is a gift of helping others, encouraging them to be better than they are, and guiding them along. Let me show you what I mean.

One of our faculty members at HCU has an extraordinary gift for exhortation, so much so that I sometimes call him "Coach". Dr. Steven Guy is a scholar and an intellectual man, but he has a knack for coaching that few people have.

If one of our students "flubs" a chapel presentation, Steven is right there exhorting and encouraging. Instead of saying, "You really messed up this morning, and you should have known better," he uses the *Next Time* principle. With an arm around the discouraged student, he gently says, "The next time you have an opportunity to present a message in chapel, you might want to consider handling it this way." Instead of crushing his heart, Steven encourages him to strive to do better–next time. Instead of criticizing, he guides him into knowing how to improve–next time.

This "coach" is a gifted exhorter. God has given him the ability to see hurt and discouragement in the heart of a student and to know the words that will encourage and build hope. Our students have benefited from Dr. Guy's gift.

❖ Giving

Some people have the gift of a green thumb. They can grow, not plants, but money. And what a gift that is! The Lord's church cannot do much of the work that she does without money. She needs money to take care of widows, orphans, the poor, and the sick. She needs to fully fund evangelism efforts. She needs many people who have a gift for giving.

I was recently in the office of a friend who is a multimillionaire. During our discussion, he related how guilty he feels because he makes so much more money than other people do.

I quickly explained to him, "That doesn't mean that God loves you more, or that you are more intelligent than others. It doesn't even mean that you work harder than most of us. It is simply that you are gifted in making money, and that gift comes from God."

A. M. Burton possessed a special gift of giving. Reared on a rural Tennessee farm and with only twenty months of formal schooling, Burton built a billion-dollar insurance company that made him a wealthy man. After becoming a Christian at age 31, he began giving away his money. During his lifetime, he personally supported hundreds of churches and educational institutions.

Upon Burton's death in 1966, Athens Clay Pullias noted in a tribute he wrote in the *Gospel Advocate* that

Burton had given more funds to a local Christian college than any Tennessean had ever given to anything. He observed that had Burton kept his money, he would have been one of the richest men in the United States. "Instead," Pullias wrote, "he gave it all away and became richer still."

All of us, of course, are participants in giving. Even the poor widow with the two mites (Mark 12:41-44) was expected to give. Everyone is included, but to some God gave in double measure the ability to make and give money. And, as is true with all of the other gifts, the gift of giving is to be used to the glory of God.

❖ **Leadership**

Some people excel at knowing where they should go and persuading other people to go with them. Those people are leaders.

Leaders can be bad or good. Adolf Hitler led an entire nation of people on a self-destructive chase to produce a superhuman race. They followed him even when it meant terminating the lives of thousands of people from another ethnic group, and even when it led to war with their global neighbors.

During that same time, however, the great English leader, Winston Churchill, was rallying his nation to give "blood, toil, tears, and sweat" in a noble fight for their homeland. I wonder whether U.S. President Harry Truman was thinking of his contemporary, Churchill, when he later defined a leader as one "who has the ability to get other people to do what they don't want to do and like it!"

In the book *Transformational Leadership*, Warren Bennis indicates that leaders have four characteristics that distinguish them. One is that they have a sharp *sense of purpose.* They know what they want to do and where they want to go. They are focused and intentional in daily living.

They also are people of *character.* Field Marshall Montgomery noted that a leader has the "character which inspires confidence." Leaders who do not have character seem to be "found out" at some point. Trying to reach a goal through selfish methods that hurt or discount others usually backfires.

Leaders are also *biased toward action.* A leader doesn't sit around waiting for someone else to do what needs to be done. A leader sees a job and takes action to get it accomplished.

Leaders are also *optimistic.* They assume that their goals can be accomplished, and they have no doubt that they can accomplish them.

The world and the church are in dire need of strong leaders. The church desperately needs men and women whose goals are in line with God's mission, who are people of deep character, and whose lives are filled with optimism.

When an inspiring, strong leader arises in the church, he or she needs to be able to use that gift of leadership to persuade others to be involved in accomplishing the great mission of the church. With just a little prodding and influence by a leader, some folks who have been initially reluctant have found themselves serving on mission fields, teaching in classrooms, serving meals to the homeless, or teaching the Scriptures to others around a dinner table. Joel Barker notes that people will follow a leader "to a place that [they] would not go by [themselves]."

Men and women who have this gift are a blessing. They can use their gift for the glory of God.

❖ Mercy

I call this gift, the gift of counseling. Some people can walk into a room full of people and immediately sense the one in that room who is lonely, or troubled, or carrying a heavy burden. While many of us are oblivious, those people seem to have radar for knowing who needs special attention. They have the gift of mercy. They are sensitive to others' needs, and they know how and what to say to hurting people.

I definitely do not have that gift. So many times, I have had foot-in-mouth disease. In fact, I have said the wrong thing at the wrong time at the wrong place so many times that I have wanted to crawl under a rug and disappear! I have asked chubby young women, who were not expecting, when the baby was due. I do not have the gift of mercy.

Through the serious illness of our young grandson, Cole, we have learned some things about mercy. We have learned that some people, although they intend to be helpful, actually say things that are hurtful and insensitive. We have also learned some helpful things from those who have the gift of mercy.

I have condensed these helps into four steps that anyone can take. Since God's people are called upon frequently to minister to those who have experienced illnesses, deaths, or tragedies of various kinds, knowing what to do helps us to bless them. The next time you are talking to someone who has just discovered that a family member has a terminal illness:

(1) Groan with them. Simply say, "Ohhhh. I am so sorry."

(2) Ask, "What is her (his) name?" Find a pen somewhere, and even if you must write the name on

your hand, write down the person's name.

(3) Say, "I will pray for (name of family member) today."

(4) Pray for the person.

These four steps can help ease the hurt of a person with a broken heart as well as enrich your prayer life. You have aligned yourself with that person in her misery. You have taken a personal interest in the family member, and you have promised to invoke the power of God on her behalf. What a blessing to hurting people! Anyone, even without the gift of mercy, can be helpful and sensitive this way.

YOUR PERSONAL GIFT(S)

So, how do you find your gift? If you pay close attention, people will often tell you what your gift is. When they tell you that you have blessed them in some way, they are guiding you toward your gift.

Sometimes, people can even tell you what your gift is NOT. We may often convince ourselves that we are good at something, but if others are silent or reluctant with compliments, then our gift may lie in other areas.

In the shower, I am one of the world's greatest male vocalists. But, in front of a crowd, I sound like Kermit the Frog on sinus medicine! Although I love to sing and join the congregation in singing with joy and enthusiasm, no one has ever told me I have the gift of singing. Their silence tells me I do not have that gift.

If you are still looking for your gifts, perhaps these questions will help:

What do you have an intense interest in?

What comes naturally to you?

What do other people tell you that you do well?

What do people NOT tell you?

What gives you the greatest sense of fulfillment?

What creates excitement and enthusiasm in you?

What gives you the sense that "this is right for me"?

Some of us may have just one gift. Others have more than a few. However many gifts you have, you are to use them. If you want to make your life count, discover and use your gift wisely to the glory of God.

Ephesians 3:20

Now to Him who is able to do exceedingly abundantly above all that we ask or think, according to the power that works in us .

In the next few pages you will discover that:

- ❖ By enlisting others' strengths, you will multiply your own.

- ❖ To empower others, you must set them free to use their abilities.

- ❖ A focus on self inhibits your strengths and abilities.

Principle Seven

ལ་ཕEmpowerOthersལ་ཕ

John Maxwell, one of the foremost experts on leadership, notes that true leaders have two main attributes. They possess the ability to lift up others and the ability to gain authority by giving it away.

Both of these attributes indicate that true leaders focus on others, not themselves. They seek to give power to others by allowing them opportunities to develop and to lead. They seemingly "step out of the way" and push others forward. They note the strengths of those around them and give responsibilities that allow others to exercise their strengths.

Although Maxwell is describing leadership in the business world, his stated principles apply easily to anyone who wants to make a difference in life. To make your life count, *enlist and empower others.*

ENLIST OTHERS

We have all known people who possess more than one individual talent. Harry Truman led the United States as President during the Second World War, but we also know that he was adept at playing the piano. Legendary college football coach, Lou Holtz, has taken numerous teams to bowl games. At the same time, however, he has provided inspiration for hundreds of people through his motivational speeches and videos.

I recently read about a young woman who had

completed an undergraduate degree in computer engineering and physics. She was headed to MIT for a doctorate in electrical engineering and computer science. Before MIT, however, she wanted to use her Rhodes scholarship for a master's degree in experimental psychology at Oxford University. She had also studied French at the Sorbonne, rowed competitively in college, and liked to listen to music in her leisure hours.

This young lady had exceptional talents and abilities, but even she has areas of limitations. She told an interviewer that she was put to shame by the political knowledge of her friends.

No matter how talented, no one can do everything well. Each of us has areas of limitations. Therefore, if you want to make your life count, enlist others who have strengths you don't have. They will fill in your gaps. Surround yourself with those who will add their strengths to yours to make a greater impact on life.

MULTIPLY YOUR EFFECTIVENESS

By enlisting the help of other people, you can multiply your effectiveness. For example, someone who has wonderful, creative ideas for Bible classes but no implementation skills can be doubly effective by asking for help from a friend who knows how to make ideas a reality. A person who has a gift for finances can greatly help another who has the ability to locate benevolent opportunities in a community. If you have a talent for knowing what to say and what should be done in a crisis, then enlisting those who know how to get it done can greatly multiply your effectiveness.

Not only will your impact be greater, but, at the same time, you will be helping others be more effective also. By teaming your strengths with others, you will help multiply the work of all.

Somehow, teaming seems to be expected in churches, civic groups, and businesses. The idea of enlisting other people seems to work better in large group settings than it does on a personal level.

Perhaps the reason is that in large groups, everybody realizes that no one person can possibly complete all the necessary tasks. Jobs cannot be completed without the help of others. No one person has all the knowledge and resources necessary to get the product made, nor does one person have enough hours in the day to complete all the work of an entire group. Enlisting help in those settings seems easy.

On a personal level, however, asking for help may be done, if it is done at all, with reluctance. There may be various reasons for this reluctance, but much of the hesitation could be from the faulty reasoning of the one who hesitates. If you are reluctant to ask for help, perhaps you are following one of these examples of poor reasoning:

a. *If I ask for help, I am admitting failure or weakness.*

b. *If I enlist someone else, then he or she may do better at the task than I will.*

c. *If I involve another person, then I may be required to give over some of the decision-making.*

d. *If I draw attention to another's strengths, my own strength may be minimized in the eyes of others.*

While none of us wants to admit to having these

thoughts, we must acknowledge that they have occurred to each of us at some time. We also must admit that a close examination shows that the focus of all of them is on *self*. They focus on maximizing *self* importance, maintaining *self* power, and highlighting *self*. As we noted at the beginning of this chapter, focusing on self is not the mark of a leader. This focus is antithetical to the Christian life.

To make a life truly count, you must focus on others. You must be concerned about their needs, their power, and their strengths. Enlisting and helping others to use their strengths can help your own life be more effective and worthwhile.

GIVE FREEDOM WITH EMPOWERMENT

I must insert this caution. Enlisting others to use their abilities does not work unless you also give them the *freedom* they need to use those strengths. This freedom is the basis of empowerment.

Empowering others means that you give them the freedom to become even more powerful. It means building them up, supplying resources they need, and supporting them in various ways while they exercise and develop their own strengths.

Empowering may require that you stay in the background as they become stronger. In fact, their ability could even outstrip yours someday. Without a doubt, empowering means that your focus is not on self. Your focus is on helping God develop another person so that his or her strength can be used in His work.

Unless you are a student of fine art, you may not have heard of the French painter, Eugene Boudin. His is not exactly a household name.

Boudin was one of the first artists to paint outdoors, a technique called *en plein air*, which enhanced the colors in his paintings. At one point in his career, he took under his wing a young artist named Claude Monet. Boudin taught and encouraged Monet in the *en plein air* technique. Monet stayed in Boudin's studio for several months, learning and being guided by the older man.

Of course, we know that the fame of the pupil eventually surpassed that of the teacher. Boudin used his own talents and skills to empower Monet to develop his personal strengths. Interestingly, Boudin himself had been mentored by the Dutch painter, Johan Jongkid, who first taught Boudin to paint outdoors.

The end result of enlisting and empowering others is that your own life is extended. When Paul wrote to Timothy, he called him his "one true son in the faith" (I Timothy 1:2). Timothy wasn't actually Paul's son. Paul had only "adopted" him or chosen him to mentor. He was going to help God "grow" Timothy into being more than he had been.

Mentoring involves coaching others as they practice their skills. It means teaching when it is called for. It means investing time and effort into the selected ones so they will grow stronger. Mentoring is an unselfish gift of empowerment.

Dr. Bill Bagents, the Vice President of Academic Affairs at HCU, is a model of one who empowers others. He is a great believer in selecting one employee to work with another employee to solve a university problem. For these pairings he often selects employees who previously may have had little to do with university decisions. Through encouraging their input and through empowering them to use their abilities, he helps them develop into more powerful people.

Not only does he pair one employee with another who needs a simple problem solved, but he then steps out of the way as they solve it. His method helps make our university stronger because he enables others to use and develop strengths that could have remained hidden.

MULTIPLY YOUR ABILITIES

While the focus of empowerment is not on self, the fact is the person who empowers others receives much in return. Besides being respected and appreciated for helping another grow, the one who empowers other people increases his own impact on life.

By choosing to mentor and empower Timothy, the apostle Paul extended his work and his reach. It was virtually impossible for Paul to be everywhere he wanted and needed to be, but Timothy, his "son in the faith", could go to places Paul could not. He could teach people Paul might never see. As he coached and trained and taught Timothy, Paul essentially was multiplying himself. At the same time, although his focus was not on self, he was ensuring that his life had greater impact.

By enlisting and empowering other people, you will multiply your own abilities. Others will help your work be done in places you will never see. They will help you reach people you will never know. They will extend your work and life beyond your grave. And because you empowered them, they will help you impact the world with a greater force than you ever could have done by yourself.

Enlist and empower others. Extend your life and make it count.

James 4:14

For what is your life? It is even a vapor that appears for a little time and then vanishes away.

In the next few pages you will discover that:

- ❖ In the latter years, being able to review a satisfying life keeps a person from despair.

- ❖ To live a satisfying life, a person needs to leave something behind for others.

Principle Eight

৯৯Leave a Legacy৶ৼ

> *"Be ashamed to die until you have scored a victory for mankind."*
>
> -Theodore P. Kalogris, Ph.D.

Abel, the son of Adam and Eve, died as a relatively young man, and his death was a violent one. Yet the Scriptures state, "...he [Abel] being dead still speaks" (Hebrews 11:4). How is it that a dead man continues to speak?

Does Abel speak because his murder was not avenged? No, God took care of that with justice and with mercy. Do his wonderful deeds and his contributions to his primitive society continue to speak to us social creatures today? He may have contributed much good to his people, but the Scriptures do not tell us that. Then does he still speak just because of his youthfulness in death? None of those, of course, are the reasons that we still hear of Abel. Scripture tells us that Abel still speaks to us today because he left something behind. Abel left a legacy of faith.

Abel made a difference with his life. Even though he died much too early, his life counted. His legacy of faith is still speaking to us, even in the twenty-first century. And that brings us to the last principle in our series. The eighth way to make sure that your life counts is to leave a legacy.

MASTERY OF TASKS

Eric Ericson, the renowned psychologist and philosopher, formulated a theory concerning the stages of an individual's life. He theorized that everyone has tasks that must be mastered at each stage of life. If the individual does not master the designated task at each stage, then life is more difficult, and he tends to display the opposite of the task.

For example, Ericson stated that the very earliest task to be mastered in infancy is trust. The most significant people in a baby's life either help or hinder the child from developing trust. If he does not acquire the mastery of that task, then he learns to develop mistrust.

In adolescence, according to this theory, the most significant task that teens must master is that of forming an individual identity. Most adolescents are consumed with learning who they are (particularly apart from their parents), how to act according to that internal image of self, and how the self should relate to others. If teens do not form (or *master*) self identity, according to the theory, then their identity is diffused. In other words, they do not know who they are.

Ericson noted eight stages of development with a corresponding number of tasks. Although his theory has been around for decades, his ideas are interesting and deserve a review. In fact, much of his theory forms a background for modern educational efforts.

THE LAST TASK

To me, the last task he theorized a person needs to master is the most significant. Perhaps the reason the last task seems so important is that it comes as a result of the mastery of the tasks in the other stages of life. Ericson theorizes that in the very last stage of life, the winter years, the elderly must master the task of *integrity of self.*

I think what he means is this: In the latter years when life is mostly looking backward, a person who has mastered this task can review a life that has come together. It is a life that is filled with good things to reflect upon and that extends itself through others. In other words, a person who has integrity of self can review her life and see a life that has counted.

She can be at peace because her years have been spent in peaceful pursuits. She can enjoy the relationships in her life because she concentrated on building them. She has earned respect and admiration because she walked in respectful and admirable ways. She can leave this earth feeling satisfied because her life is a path for others to follow. A person such as that has left a legacy. And after she is gone, she will continue to speak.

DESPAIR

The reverse of that is true, also, according to Ericson's theory. The person who has not mastered tasks at the appropriate stages will be facing a life of despair in the last years.

How often is that true! A man who has gambled away his life in pursuit of power, money, or status comes to the last years. His family is gone, he never hears from his children, he made no time for friends, and business associates lasted only as long as he could help them.

The last years of his life are lonely and bitter. He

focused on things of little substance while ignoring relationships with God, with his family, and with neighbors and friends. Despair settles in.

A woman who spends years estranged from her original family, or involved in an adulterous affair, or in hostile conflict with co-workers comes at last to the winter of her life. In those last years, instead of enjoying warm friendships and family life, she is alone and without intimate relationships. No matter how much she pursues, she cannot find a life that is balanced and full of integrity. Despair is her companion.

Neither of these people can leave a desirable legacy, a path to follow for those behind. When they die, they will not continue to speak. Their lives have not counted. No matter how rich or famous or powerful they were, they did not make a significant difference in life.

LEAVE A LEGACY

If your life is to count, you must leave something behind. You must leave a legacy.

What comes to mind when you read the word *legacy*? Money or inherited material goods? A gift from a deceased relative? Bank account funds from a favorite aunt?

While all of these "treasures" can indeed be legacies in our earthly sense, the only lasting, true legacy comes from the treasure pictured vividly in the Scriptures.

Isaiah 33:6 indicates that a real treasure is the "fear of the Lord". How much better it is to "pass on" an eternal legacy of love and respect for God than to leave a temporary treasure of material goods that are soon consumed!

Wise persons who have been good stewards of God's blessings often leave legacies of material goods to their children and grandchildren. They know that those descendants will use the proceeds to do good works. Some individuals continue to ensure that the gospel will be preached by leaving legacies to the church, or to a favorite mission area, or to schools that train preachers.

Heritage Christian University has been the recipient of material legacies from a number of wise and visionary people. By helping our university train men and women to minister to others, those "legacy leavers" are multiplying their efforts all over the world. They are ensuring that the gospel will continue to be preached for generations. Those good folks will "speak beyond the grave".

Some people help to build homes for orphans or facilities that take care of the poor or sick. Their material blessings continue to bless others for generations. These "legacy leavers" will take a last breath knowing that because they concentrated on the real and eternal treasure here, they have laid up substantial treasures in heaven.

YOUR LEGACY

Have you considered what the legacy of your life will be? What will your children, your grandchildren, your neighbors and friends, your community, and the church "inherit" from your life? A wise person who has made his or her life count leaves a legacy of goodness, kindness, self-control, godliness, love, and appropriate care of material blessings.

Individuals who leave that kind of legacy continue to speak even after they are long gone from the earth. If your life is to count, leave the right kind of legacy.

The Bridge Builder

An old man, going a lone highway,
Came, at the evening, cold and gray,
To a chasm, vast, and deep, and wide,
Through which was flowing a sullen tide.

The old man crossed in the twilight dim;
The sullen stream had no fears for him;
But he turned, when safe on the other side,
And built a bridge to span the tide.

"Old man," said a fellow pilgrim near,
"You are wasting strength with building here;
Your journey will end with the ending day;
You never again must pass this way;
You have crossed the chasm, deep and wide—
Why build you a bridge at the eventide?"

The builder lifted his old gray head:
"Good friend, in the path I have come," he said,
"There followeth after me today,
A youth, whose feet must pass this way.

This chasm, that has been naught to me,
To that fair-haired youth may a pitfall be.
He, too, must cross in the twilight dim;
Good friend, I am building the bridge for him."

– Will Allen Dromgoole

Ecclesiastes 12:13

Let us hear the conclusion of the whole matter: Fear God and keep His commandments, for this is man's all.

In the next few pages you will discover that:

- ❖ Many people at the end of life wish they had spent their time more wisely.

- ❖ You can incorporate the eight principles into your days and watch your life change.

Conclusion

❧A Satisfied Mind❧

How many times have you heard someone say,
"If I had his money I could do things my way."

But little they know, that it's so hard to find,
One rich man in ten with a satisfied mind.

Once I was winning in fortune and fame,
Everything that I dreamed for to get a start in life's game.

The suddenly it happened, I lost every dime,
But I'm richer by far with a satisfied mind.

Money can't buy back your youth when you're old,
Or a friend when you're lonely or a love that's grown cold.

The wealthiest person is a pauper at times,
Compared to the man with a satisfied mind.

When my life has ended and my time has run out,
My friends and my loved ones, I'll leave there's no doubt.

But one thing's for certain, when it comes my time,
I'll leave this old world with a satisfied mind.

– Satisfied Mind,
Red Hayes and Jack Rhodes
Starrite Music

I think all of us would like to leave this earth with a satisfied mind. But what is it that leads to satisfaction with our lives?

I once read about the results of a survey of people who had lived past age 100. One of the questions the interviewers asked was, "If you had your life to live over again, what would you do differently?"

When the results were compiled, three answers seemed to occur frequently. The elderly people said they wish they had done these three things more often.

REFLECTION

They said that if they could live life again, they would *reflect more.* They would think more about what they were doing. They would meditate more about ideas and their own actions. They would ponder more about events and other people.

Someone once told me that people must not learn from experience because they keep repeating the same mistakes again and again. I would have to agree that many people do seem to have blinders on when they make a mistake. They do not seem to reflect on the cause, their actions, or the circumstances that surround it.

These are people that *live and live only.* They may live through all kinds of circumstances and situations. Devastating things may happen to them, many of which are even the result of their own actions. For a while they may be a little shell-shocked, but they eventually get over it.

Then something else happens, and they are stunned again and grasp for straws to hold to. After a time, however, they just go on living. I notice, though, that each time something happens, a person like that seems to lose some part of self that is intangible. It may be a bit of his spirit or a piece of hope or even his health.

LIVING A WORTHWHILE LIFE

Besides just living and letting life happen to him, there are other ways for a person to live. I want to mention four of them that can make your life worthwhile:

❖ Life can be worthwhile if you *live and learn.*

But... it is not the experience that teaches you. According to Warren Bennis, people do not learn from experience; they learn from their *reflection* on that experience.

Experience does not cause you to grow in wisdom and maturity. Your *reflection* on the experience causes you to grow whether the experience is positive or negative.

A man who survives his first heart attack has an opportunity to become a healthy, old person. That is, he does if he reflects on that experience and learns from it. If he goes about his life as he once did, perhaps eating rich foods, being a couch potato, or continuing to work in a stressful job, he may soon have another heart attack or other health problems.

A man who reflects on that negative health experience and learns from it, however, is likely to make changes that promote his health and a longer life. He decides to eat healthier foods, to exercise faithfully, and to search for relief from too much stress. If he does so, he is more likely to have good experiences in the future than one who doesn't.

A man like that can enjoy the rewards of learning

lessons that improve his health and his life. At the same time, he can begin to be more satisfied with the tenor and content of his life.

If a woman with a fear of public speaking makes a successful work presentation for a roomful of people, she can learn from that positive situation. She can reflect on her fear, the fact that she faced her fear, and the things she did well. She can also think about what she will need to do next time.

Life will be easier for her the next time the same circumstance arises. She has grown by her reflection on the experience.

I wonder if this kind of learning was what the 100-year-old people had in mind when they indicated they would reflect more. Somehow, I think they did .

❖ Life can be worthwhile if you *try*.

It is not enough just to learn something; you also must try. Try to make some progress. Try to learn a new skill. Try to behave in a more positive manner. Try.

Suppose I place a bar two feet off the ground and ask a group of kids to jump the bar. Some would be able to and some would not. If I raised it another six inches, some could still jump it, some might knock the bar down, but some would not even try.

If those who knocked down the bar had another opportunity to jump, some of them would not attempt it, but others would try harder and succeed. They might get a deeper breath, they might start with more energy, or they might lift their legs differently. Not only did they learn from their first attempt, but they were willing to try again.

Life can be worthwhile for those who give every

effort. They can have success because they try .

❖ Life can be worthwhile if you *stay*.

I remember once watching a man put in a foundation for a house. He finished the foundation, but I didn't see the walls go up. In fact, the foundation is all he ever completed. Weeds soon took over the lot and grew taller than the foundation.

I don't know if the man had financial difficulties or if he just had trouble *staying*. Life is more worthwhile for those who stay.

If you agree to a project, see it through. If you sign up for the season, stay until the finish. If you guarantee you will be there for harvest, then prepare the soil, plant the seeds, and stay until the reaping is done.

When you commit to anything that is worthy, stay until the finish. That applies to work, to marriage, to parenting, and to church. There is no reward for those who quit part of the way through. Rewards come at the reaping.

The reaping may bring promotions and a pleasant work environment for those who follow through. Rewards for marital "stick-to-it-iveness" may be celebrating your fiftieth wedding anniversary and watching your children's children grow to adulthood. For those who have committed their lives to Christ and stay regardless of worldly circumstances, rewards can be spiritual growth and becoming more like Christ.

Rewards come for those who stay. The reaping is worth it all.

❖ Life can be worthwhile if you *care*.

If you care at all, you will get some results. If you

care enough, the results can be incredible, even life-changing.

Caring enough means getting involved in whatever is noble, honorable, true, and praiseworthy. It means getting your hands dirty to help someone else.

It may mean housing a homeless family temporarily. It could mean emptying your wallet to help build a church building in a foreign country. Caring might mean helping to support a missionary with your money and your encouragement. It might even mean teaching the gospel yourself to people who are vastly different from you.

People who care enough will do any or all of those things. They will do those things because they care enough to make a difference. Caring enough can make your life worthwhile.

RISK-TAKING

The 100-year-olds who were interviewed also said they would *risk* more if they could live life again. They would take more chances. They would step out in faith. Because their lives were winding down and they had the advantage of looking back through the long corridor of years, they wished they had taken more risks.

I have observed that there are two kinds of risks: foolish risks and calculated risks. Foolish risks are those that are taken with no forethought, no planning, and no gathering of information. We call it "jumping in."

That phrase brings to mind the image of a young boy who approaches an unknown swimming hole, strips off his clothes, and dives in. He doesn't know how deep the water is.

He doesn't know if there are tree roots, if the bottom is filled with gravel, or if there is a large piece of concrete sunk in the creek bed. What a foolish risk he could be taking. Frequently, as we know, foolish risks cause a great deal of pain, sometimes life-long pain.

On the other hand, calculated risks are those that are carefully investigated, mulled over, and deemed worthwhile. An elderly person once told me, "You see that property over there? I could have bought that once for 27 cents an acre, but I was afraid I couldn't pay for it. Now it's worth over $2 million."

I wonder if he had gathered information about the property and its surroundings. Had he studied the history of economic depressions? Did he know about the ups and downs of the national economy? Did he get the advice of those who had done similar things?

If he had gathered all the information and then decided to hand over the money for the property (that is, if he had the money during depressed times), he would have taken a calculated risk. The purchase would still be a risk, but the likelihood of succeeding would be much higher.

None of us wants to take foolish risks, but a person who takes a calculated risk frequently succeeds. When he does, people often describe him as a person with "good judgment."

The older people wistfully said they wished they had taken more risks. I think they must have been thinking about opportunities they let pass by. At the time of the survey, they regretted that they had not seized those opportunities.

CONCENTRATION ON THINGS THAT ENDURE

They indicated they also would *concentrate on things that last*. Many of the things in life do not last. All the material goods that surround our lives will not last. Houses, cars, clothes, everything that is bought and sold will not last. We can be replaced in the positions we hold in our jobs. The companies we work for will not last. They merge and buy out and go out of business. Our hobbies and recreation, while pleasant and sometimes necessary to our lives, will not last.

The intangible things in life are those that last. Relationships and spiritual matters are enduring. Those are the things that are ultimately important. Building relationships with family members, with friends, and with members of the church family should be high on our priority list. A focus on spiritual growth, both our own and that of others, is a lasting effort that will go with us into eternity.

I heard about a family who went back to their grandmother's house after attending the older woman's funeral. Family members went carefully and tearfully through the house looking at all the things that grandmother cherished. They came upon an unframed needlepoint sampler draped across the arm of her rocking chair. It was the last thing the old woman had done. A granddaughter picked it up and read the adage on the sampler: "Days will come, days will pass. What's done with love will last."

Through that needlepoint work, Grandmother was telling her family what was important. Much of what we do daily is unimportant and will soon be forgotten. Our days pass rapidly, but the intangible things last.

Love, joy, and service are important. The service and love we extend to God are vital. Those things are lasting. At her advanced age, Grandmother had learned what was

94

important.

YOUR PERSONAL ANSWER

How would you answer the question from the survey? What would you do differently if you could live your life again?

Would you say that you would spend more time with your family? Or that you would go into a different career?

Perhaps, like the old people who were interviewed, you would concentrate on more important things this time. You would focus more on the intangibles.

The good news is this: You don't have to live your life again to do things differently. You can start right now where you are. No matter your age, no matter your family situation, and no matter your health or financial condition, you can turn away from an unfocused life. You don't have to drift wherever circumstances take you. Today you can begin to make your life count.

MAKING YOUR LIFE COUNT

You can change your life today. You can begin to make a difference in the world. Follow the eight principles explained in the preceding chapters of this book, and you will begin to notice your life taking on purpose and meaning.

First, *believe that you will live forever*. No life is unimportant. Your own life will not have an end... ever! That principle is absolutely primary to a purposeful life. Knowing you will live forever gives you a different perspective. It begins to hone and shape your life.

Second, *accept your mortality and get comfortable*

with it. Fully understand that, while your soul will live forever, your body will die someday. That understanding gives you a sense of urgency about the time you have on earth. You realize time is short and precious and is not to be wasted.

Next, *determine to change the world with the time you have.* The first step in changing the world is to change yourself. As you begin to make small changes, in an action or a reply or a tone of voice, you will notice others around you begin to change. You are on the way to changing the world.

Fourth, *take personal responsibility for your life.* Be responsible for the way you live. Surrender to God the things in life that you cannot control, and take responsibility for those things you can. God has given you control over your own behavior, your attitude, the goals you set, and the decisions you make. He allows you complete control over decisions about a life mate and about a career. He gives you the freedom to choose for whom you live and whether you will serve self or others. Take responsibility for those decisions.

Fifth, *develop a sense of purpose.* A life purpose guides your days, it controls your decisions, and it forms your mission. A sense of purpose lets you know you are not here by accident. There is a reason for your existence, and God made you for that purpose. That kind of feeling helps you wake each morning to find the opportunities and challenges of the day.

Sixth, *find and develop your gifts.* Your particular talents and abilities are not the same as those of anyone else. Your gender, your personality, and your culture combine with natural, God-given abilities to create a uniqueness of strengths that are yours alone. Those gifts can be developed to be used in service to God and His people.

Seven, *empower other people.* Your own life, your abilities, and your work can be extended through enlisting others and giving them the freedom to use their strengths. Their strengths, combined with yours, help you to be more effective. By empowering others, you can create momentum that lasts long after you are gone.

Last, *leave a legacy.* A good legacy blesses others and helps them remember you after you are gone. Their memory of your well-lived life means that you changed the world in a positive way. Your work and service made a difference in the lives of others. What you did and what you said contributed to their good in some way. Determine to leave a legacy that makes your world a better place than you found it.

NOW WHAT?

Those are the eight principles. They are simple and concise. None of them is difficult, but all of them can be life-changing.

Will you commit to them right now? I can promise that if you fully accept these principles and begin working on them, things will begin to happen. You will first notice small changes.

If you commit to following through on incorporating these principles into your life, the small changes will increase until your entire life is different. Your perspective, your attitude, your purpose, your relationships, and your actions will have new meaning. You will be more satisfied and have a sense of fulfillment. Your life will take on purpose. You will know that you are here for a reason.

When it happens that your time on earth is over, you can know that your life made a difference. You can leaf through the pages of your life and see the purpose and discipline that formed the days. You can review the ways you used your talents. You can remember those that you helped to develop their own abilities. You can see that your life's work has been extended through others.

You can leave this earth knowing that you are leaving an excellent legacy behind. You can have the satisfaction that comes from knowing your life has been lived well. You will have lived a life that counts.

What Will Matter

Ready or not, some day it will all come to an end.
There will be no more surprises, no minutes, hours or days.
All the things you collected, whether treasured or forgotten,
   will pass to someone else.
Your wealth, fame and temporal power will shrivel to
   irrelevance.
It will not matter what you owned or what you were owed.
Your grudges, resentments, frustrations, and jealousies will
   finally disappear.
So too, your hopes, ambitions, plans and to-do lists will
   expire.
It won't matter where you came from or what side of the
   tracks you lived on at the end.
It won't matter whether you were beautiful or brilliant.
Even your gender and skin color will be irrelevant.
So what will matter? How will the value of your days be
   measured?
What will matter is not what you bought but what you built,

Not what you got but what you gave.
What will matter is not your success but your significance.
What will matter is not what you learned but what you taught.
What will matter is every act of integrity, compassion, courage or sacrifice that enriched, empowered or encouraged others to emulate your example.
What will matter is not your competence but your character.
What will matter is not how many people you knew, but how many will feel a lasting loss when you are gone.
What will matter is not your memories but the memories that live in those who loved you.
What will matter is how long you will be remembered, by whom and for what.
Living a life that matters doesn't happen by accident.
It's not a matter of circumstance but of choice.
Choose to live a life that matters.

- Michael Josephson © 2003

❧❧*Appendix A*❧❧

THE GOAL SETTING PROCESS

The following step-by-step process will speed your movement toward desired goals.

1. **Have a strong desire.** The stronger the desire, the more likely you will reach your goal.

2. **Believe you can accomplish your goals.** What your mind can conceive and believe, you can achieve.

3. **Write down your goals.** An unwritten goal is no goal at all.

4. **Determine how you will benefit from accomplishing your goal.** The more benefits you can write down, the more likely you will be successful.

5. **Analyze your position.** You cannot get to the place you want to go until you know where your starting point is.

6. **Set a deadline for the accomplishment of your goal.** A goal is a dream with a deadline.

7. **Identify the obstacles that must be overcome.** There are always obstacles. The more you know about them the better prepared you are to face them.

8. **Clearly identify the knowledge you will need.** Knowledge is power and will accelerate your progress.

9. **Clearly identify the people whose cooperation**

and assistance you will need. There is an abundance of help available. Use it!

10. **Take all the details in the last three steps and make a plan.** Without a plan you cannot become aware when you are off course.

11. **Mentally visualize the goal as already attained.** Think, act, walk, and talk as if you are the person you want to be.

12. **Back your plan with determination and persistence.** Never, never, never give up.

13. **Learn effective time management.** You have as many hours in a day as anyone else. Use them to move closer to your goal.

14. **Keep your eye on the prize.** Always think about your goal. Keep yourself up!

❧❧*Appendix B*❧❧

FINDING YOUR PRIORITIES

If you are trying to overcome barriers to achieve your goals but find yourself getting stuck, try the following techniques:

- Pretend that you have only six months to live. What do you want to accomplish in that short time?

  List five (5) things.

- Pretend that you just received $10 million tax free. Now that money is no object, what do you want to accomplish?

  List five (5) things.

- Pretend you must write your own obituary. What will you write?

  Write five (5) sentences.

❧❧Appendix C❧❧

A Psalm of Life

Tell me not in mournful numbers,
Life is but an empty dream
For the soul is dead that slumbers
And things are not what they seem.

Life is real! Life is earnest!
And the grave is not its goal;
Dust thou art, to dust returnest
Was not spoken of the soul.

Not enjoyment, and not sorrow,
Is our destined end or way;
But to act, that each to-morrow
Find us farther than to-day.

Art is long and Time is fleeting,
And our hearts, though stout and brave,
Still, like muffled dreams, are beating
Funeral marches to the grave.

In the world's broad field of battle,
In the bivouac of life,
Be not like dumb, driven cattle!
Be a hero in the strife!

Trust no future, howe'er pleasant!
Let the dead Past bury its dead!
Act! – act within the present!
Heart within, and God o'erhead!

Lives of great men all remind us
We can make our lives sublime
And, departing, leave behind us
Footprints on the sands of time;

Footprints that perhaps another,
Sailing o'er life's solemn main
A forlorn and shipwrecked brother,
Seeing, shall take heart again.

Let us, then, be up and doing,
With a heart for any fate,
Still achieving, still pursuing,
Learn to labor and to wait.

– Henry Wadsworth Longfellow

❧❧*About the Author*❧❧

Dennis Jones, a graduate of Heritage Christian University and Murray State University, is in his twenty-second year as president of Heritage Christian University. He has been preaching for 37 years and has conducted over 300 gospel meetings and seminars.

President Jones is a much sought-after speaker on the subjects of evangelism, family, leadership, and Christian attitudes. His interpersonal communications course at HCU continues to be popular with students. He and his wife, Fredda, have three children and eight grandchildren and live in Florence, Alabama.